Richard Glover

The Substance of the Evidence

Delivered to a Committee of the Honourable House of Commons by the

Merchants and Traders of London, concerned in the trade to Germany and

Holland, and of the dealers in foreign linens

Richard Glover

The Substance of the Evidence
Delivered to a Committee of the Honourable House of Commons by the Merchants and Traders of London, concerned in the trade to Germany and Holland, and of the dealers in foreign linens

ISBN/EAN: 9783337189235

Printed in Europe, USA, Canada, Australia, Japan

Cover: Foto ©Suzi / pixelio.de

More available books at **www.hansebooks.com**

THE
SUBSTANCE
OF THE
EVIDENCE

Delivered to a COMMITTEE of the

Honourable HOUSE of COMMONS

BY THE

MERCHANTS and TRADERS of London,

Concerned in the

TRADE to GERMANY and HOLLAND,

AND OF THE

DEALERS in FOREIGN LINENS,

As Summed up

By Mr. GLOVER.

To which is Annexed,

HIS SPEECH,

INTRODUCTORY TO THE

PROPOSALS

Laid before the ANNUITANTS of

Meſſ. DOUGLAS, HERON and Co.

At the KING's-ARMS Tavern, Cornhill, on the Ninth
of *February*, 1774.

LONDON:

Printed for J. WILKIE, St. Paul's Church-Yard.
M DCC LXXIV.

[Price One Shilling and Six-pence.]

THE

SUBSTANCE

OF THE

EVIDENCE, &c.

WHEN I firſt had the honour of ad-
miſſion at this Bar, I prefaced the
Examination under my particular care with
an aſſertion, that no queſtion of higher national import could come before you; that the
very baſis of this kingdom's ſtability and
power was concerned in your inveſtigation,
and the future deciſion of Parliament upon
your report. It reſts upon me to make the
aſſertion good. With all due attention to the
evidence I have examined, I ſhall take my
principal ſtand upon the report of laſt year,
made public by the authority of this Houſe.
I ſhall not to my knowledge quote any con-
trovertible fact; deductions and concluſions

rank under another predicament. The Report
fets forth a decline in the Britifh and Irifh
manufacture of Linen, and the numerous
emigrations, of your people; facts which, I
admit: but that they are imputable to an increafed import of foreign Linens, or to any
abufe in thofe imports, is a conclufion I to-
tally difpute. Having therefore admitted the
evil, and rejected the caufe affigned; I feel it
incumbent upon me to fearch for the real one,
upon whofe difcovery the main of this queftion in the firft inftance abfolutely depends.
Briefly, Sir, the method I fhall purfue is to
fhew, what has been the genuine caufe of the
evil, what has not, and what is not the remedy.
I will then difclofe the nature, depth and extent of the malady, not hitherto fully repre-
fented to you; the quarter, where it ftill con-
tinues confuming the vitals there, and threat-
ning more mifchief to the whole; and I will
conclude with fuggefting under your permif-
fion the only radical cure.

The caufe, Sir, unparralleled fince the firft
intercourfe between Nation and Nation, of a
calamity fo feverely felt by three kingdoms,
and

and the quarter, whence it took its rife, and
made its progrefs over all; will require a narrative, founded on that material part of Mr.
Payne's Evidence relative to the general ftagnation of credit; a narrative neceffary for
your Information, concife I could wifh, accurate I truft, undeniably true I know; and
fuch, that if the manner could equal the
matter, would lift your attention to aftonifhment. In all commercial nations, whenever
moderation and frugality have yielded to ex-
travagance and ambition, wants have been
created, which common profits could not fupply; thofe wants have been the parents of
projects, and a rafh, afpiring fpirit of enter-
prife has overborne the fober temper of regular trade. This reftlefs and intemperate fpirit
has been predominant among one people, diftinguifhed by a feries and variety of recent
projects concerted without knowledge, without forecaft, without fyftem, executed by
rafhnefs, terminating in ruin, almoft total to
themfelves, and detriment almoft general a-
mong their fuffering neighbours. It is from
this quarter, we have feen ftupendous under-

taking

takings in buildings, in the cultivation of re-
mote iflands, in manufactures upon no other
certainty, than an enormous and infupportable
expence. It is from this quarter, we
have feen projects of avarice, of rapacity,
productive of mifery and depopulation under
the miftaken name of improvements. It is
from this quarter, that the great markets of
trade have been glutted by wild commercial
adventurers under the delufion of a temporary
but falfe capital : but above all, the banking
adventure is filled moft with the marvellous.
That part I fhall not detail merely to avoid an
imputation readily thrown upon me, an imputation of amufing the committee with poetic
fiction ; but thus much I muft fay, in one period, that if a certain celebrated Spanifh author
could revive to exhibit his hero under the new
character of a banker, he might fpare his in-
vention every kind of labour, as recent and indubitable facts in our own ifland could furnifh
incidents, every one at leaft upon a par with
his windmills : yet, Sir, could that moft fagaci-
ous perfon travel over that land of projects
and converfe with its inhabitants, he would
find

find amongft them, erudition and fcience, jurifprudence, theology, hiftory, oratory.---in fhort, Sir, every fenfe but that common fort, upon which all worldly welfare both public and private depends, by a juft application of the elements of trade, manufactures, money and credit to rational and practical Improvements, a fyftem yet to be learned by that fcientific, lettered and eloquent nation. Sir, I will now effay to excite your aftonifhment; thefe numerous undertakings, I think juftly termed ftupendous, were attempted, nearly at once in the fame period, were carried on at an expence of fums incredible, and yet the projectors had no capital of their own. They had, Sir, I prefume, a fecond fight of immenfe acquifitions, and one would think purfued their plan by fome fupernatural aid. Sir, what they did will not be credible to pofterity; the univerfe never furnifhed a people that ever made fuch a gigantic attempt at the attribute of Omnipotence in creation ; abfolutely they created millions of money out of nothing; by a certain alchymy, which they poffeffed, they extracted millions of hard money

out

out of the pliant purse of their neighbours, and at the same time ruined themselves. This operation, Sir, is called Paper Circulation.

My honourable hearers are above the want or use of such an operation; to suppose them therefore unacquainted with it, I mean a compliment to them and an apology for myself in giving some brief explanation of it.

A knot of projectors at one end of the island send up immeasurable quantities of this enchanted paper to their brethren, their countrymen, projectors like themselves, settled at the other end. These, Sir, by their magical tip of the pen, called acceptance and indorsement, instantly converted this paper into money to any amount by what is called discount; the first produce was instantly absorbed by the projects in hand, a second must be provided equal to the first, to discharge the first set of bills when due; else the spell would be immediately broken: A second set was sent up and converted into money in the same way, and applied to discharge the first. A third, the second, a fourth the third, and so on.

Children in sport can make a circulation
upon

upon water by the caft of a ftone, and by that
repetition can keep it up for a while ; but the
child knows, he cannot make it everlafting:
this was not known to the man of the North,
whofe infatuation adopted the chimera of the
South-fea year, that credit was infinite. For
example ; Sir, one fpciety only in the midft of
all this defolation, which remains to be
defcribed, had drained a certain capital of fix
hundred thoufand pounds in hard money, in
exchange for a nominal value in paper ; it coft
them about nine per cent. to raife that fum in
order to be lent out at five : and there were
: among their managers, who looked upon this,
Sir, as profit (nobody will difpute what I fay
upon this head) and that the more this paper
was extended the better, a bubble, fcarce to
be matched in the 1720, of one country, and
in defpite of all experience then, or fince, re-
ferved to diftinguifh the other in 1772. In
fhort, Sir, fuch was the inexplicable coincidence
of circumftances, that what with the intrepid
perfeverance of one kingdom, in borrowing,
and what with the torpid facility of the other
in lending, a chain of circulation was eftablifhed,

lifhed, which comprehended both the capitals
and moft of the intermediate places; a chain
growing in fize weekly and daily, induring
for the two whole Years 1770 and 1771 down
to June 1772, when one link gave way---the
charm was inftantly diffolved, leaving behind
it confternation in the place of confidence,
and imaginary affluence changed to real want
and diftrefs; a torrent of ruin from the North,
forced a paffage into your capital, into the
moft fecret depofitories of treafure; a run was
felt by your bankers, fucceffive falls of houfes
in trade, eminent at leaft for the wildnefs and
immenfity of their tranfactions, became the
daily, the hourly news; an univerfal diffidence
enfued; credit feemed withering to the root;
a general ftagnation prevailed in every branch
of trade and manufacture; the commercial
genius of your ifland languifhed in every part.
For a fingle manufacture in that part, whence
the evil took its rife, to have efcaped would
have been a wonder bordering upon prodigy,
none to have fhared the common lot of all from
a grievous and popular diftemper, arifing
from that quarter the moft reftlefs of all,
                                          when

when its unfatisfied and intemperate ambition
gave wing to that black fwarm of projects,
which at once overfpread three kingdoms, like
one of the ten plagues. Sir, I have pointed
out a fact of public notoriety, the quarter
whence the evil came ; but as a farther con-
firmation, among the millions ftagnated, or
loft, in confequence of failures in that fatal
period, four fifths in value are directly
chargeable upon the natives of that quarter;
and of the remaining fifth, the greateft part
fell among thofe unfortunate men of this kingdom, who had connections with the other.

Sir, there is no exaggeration in this de-
fcription. I fhould have reafon to boaft of my
own powers, could I give a perfect picture of
the diftrefs at that time ; might I refer to the
teftimony of one, who by his fituation that
year muft have been better informed, than
any other perfon, he beft knew the terror
which oppreffed all men, when he produced
the palladium of public credit, depofited by
the ftate, in the cuftody of that moft illuftrious corporation, the Bank of England ; he
there diftinguifhed himfelf. I hope no man

C

ever

ever will have an occafion to do more. It was
he, he and his brethren, though they could not
prevent the mifchief already done, ufed their
utmoft endeavours, looking ftill to that country, whence the evil took its rife. I was myfelf a fubaltern upon the occafion, ufing my
feeble endeavours to refcue that country from
its own fuicide hand. Sir, he confeffedly at
that time faved the principal commercial town
of that country; that eye of Scotland, by ftrain-
ing at a view too extenfive, had been extinguifhed
without the affiftance of that witnefs, who when
firft introduced at your Bar appeared fo hurt, as
a gentleman and as a merchant, at certain Infinuations thrown out upon the whole trade. Sir,
neither Mr. Payne, nor myfelf, the fecond
oftenfible perfon upon this occafion, could
look upon ourfelves but as above any fuch
imputation; but it is not in our power to fhut
the mouth of national prejudice; there may
be thoufands, whom we cannot controul, who
may charge thefe and many more afperfions
thrown out during this proceeding, with the
imputation of containing in them an illiberal

and

and ferocious tincture, verging on barbarifm. I have now undeniably afcertained the genuine caufe of the calamity, which is known to be general, and the quarter whence it folely took its rife.

Next, Sir, there is another calamity, which is, I cannot help faying, undauntedly afcribed to the increafed import of foreign Linen, the emigration from one kingdom at leaft, confifting of hufbandmen and peafants, men altogether unconnected with manufactures. Sir, I hope I have not tired you with narrative. I am very unfortunate if I do; for above half my difcourfe will be hiftorical. I muft give you a fhort narrative now by way of interrogation. I afk, whether not more than twenty hufbandmen of fome property in one of the weftern iflands, in the northernmoft part of this country, did not make the firft emigration to avoid an increafe of rents, which appeared to them exorbitant; and drew after them many hundreds of inferior perfons, never to return more? Did not fome hundreds in another of the weftern iflands fly from the oppreffion of factors and doers, that is agents

and

and ftewards, of a much injured and noble
proprietor, himfelf excelling in merit and ac-
complifhments? Did not fome hundreds in
Sutherland fly from a new oppreffion under an
Hebrew Tribe, called Tackmen, Leffees, as
is the cafe in Ireland, of large Tracts of land,
who find a profit in grinding the hard labour-
ing man? They, Sir, had the audacity to
revive perfonal fervice in imitation of the Cor-
vees in France, where days work are exacted
from the vaffal to the lord. Sir, I had all this
in the country itfelf. I will afk them, whether
a Farmer by the name of James Hogg of
Borlum, near Thurfoe in Caithnefs, did not
laft November embark with two hundred
more and winter in the Orkneys, remaining
there for a frefh fhip from Leith to profecute
their voyage to North Carolina, never to re-
vifit their old habitations, though feparated
from them at no greater diftance than Pent-
land *Firth*. After this a phrenfy of emigration became epidemical in Invernefs and Mur-
ray fhire; many embarked for America, who
had no caufe of complaint againft their fupe-
riors. As I was told, they went upon a principle

ciple of pride to North America, expecting
to become Lairds themselves in that suppofed
paradife : I almoft repeat the words I heard
at Edinburgh, and feveral other places. Sir,
the fame phrenfy penetrated to Rofsfhire, upon
a vaft tract of land poffeffed by a gentleman,
illuftrious for his gallant and meritorious fer-
vices in the military line, not lefs meritorious
now in his retirement, devoted to civilize and
cultivate his country : his difcretion equal to
his humanity by condefcending to reafon with
his inferiors in their own mode, reconciled
them to the comfortable fituation of tenants
under him : but if his example is not fol-
lowed, emigration will take place and aug-
ment year after year ; and, I hope, without
offence I may recommend the fame example
to Ireland. Sir, I will likewife recommend
my honourable hearers to an Highland difcourfe
upon this fubject tranfmitted to me
from Scotland, which more forcibly and more
pathetically afcribes this emigration to the
fame caufes I do, fuperadding one of his
own infinitely beyond my reach, that this
fpirit is infufed by Divine vengeance to chaf-
tife

tife avarice and cruelty. And thus, Sir, I have endeavoured to fhew, what has been the caufe of this evil.

But now, Sir, the authors of all thefe evils, with no other fenfation, than of their local diftrefs, concealing, that their wounds were given by their own fuicide hands, without compunction for the mifery brought on two fifter kingdoms by fo many unwarrantable and pernicious projects, have taken the field a fecond time upon a new adventure, which I will prove hurtful to themfelves and the public : but let them not think, that their march has been in difguife by placing an Englifh manufacture in their van. Sir, I honour the individual induftry of that manufacture, as much as in the greateft ; but I am fatisfied, no Englifh Gentleman can be difpleafed, when I tell him, that the utmoft annual value of that manufacture, to the higheft amount of their own ftating in the printed report, is not a five hundredth part of the woollen ; nor can they conceal under the name of another kingdom, quiet and contented in itfelf from the encouragement already received, no ways ad-
dicted

dicted to projects, knowing, experienced and
regular in their trade, I say that under that
name they muft not think to conceal that im-
petuofity, which has brought them forward
again, and has fixed them upon a ground of
allegation and calculation diametrically re-
pugnant to the truth of figures. I believe I
muft now trouble you with a little calculation.

Mr. Payne, Sir, delivered to the committee
moft accurate calculations of foreign imports
at feveral periods----a paper (N° 12) in the
printed report will fufficiently fhew the fluctuation of trade. I, when afked as a Hamburgh
merchant, what the quantity of yards might
be at a medium, have always anfwered, that
for many years they have amounted to twenty-
five millions of yards a year, not meaning,
that every year was alike : and one, who
judges of trade by the higheft year, and another by the loweft, would be both equally
miftaken, and ever remain in the dark. Ac-
cidents common or uncommon, occafion
thefe variations. This paper (N° 12) a paper
of their own, Sir, (I hope, I fhall not be
guilty of any thing clandeftine in making ufe
of

of any thing from their own papers againft them) this paper exhibits the imports for twenty years, from Chriftmas 1751 to Chriftmas 1771; to form a comparative judgment of trade, you fhould always take large periods. In the firft ten years the imports amounted to three hundred millions of yards, or 30,000,000 at an annual medium. The laft period of ten years amounted to two hundred and fifty mil-lions of yards, or twenty-five millions at an annual medium. Now, Sir, it feems to me, that this is a decreafe of five millions of yards; and that twenty-five, is lefs than thirty by five. They call this an increafe; it is not the firft time they and I have differed about the mean-ing of words. The quantity of Irifh linen in the firft period is a hundred and thirty millions of yards, in the laft period one hundred and eighty millions. This I call an increafe, in the laft period of fifty millions, or five millions a year. The quantity of Scotch linen ftampt for fale in the firft period is ninety-nine milli-ons of yards; in the laft one hundred and and twenty-feven millions. An increafe of twenty-eight millions, or two millions eight
hundred

hundred thoufand yards a year. I, Sir, who have been intimately converfant with a certain new race of calculators upon a former occafion, do fufpect, that upon the prefent occafion, they have lent fome of their fkill to the Irifh; nor am I in the leaft furprized at my differing with them in the meaning of decreafe and increafe; we never could agree upon the fenfe of the words profit and lofs: for, Sir, no warning, no advice, no argument could perfuade thefe calculators, that lending out at Five per cent. money, which ftood them in Nine, was an Operation directly the reverfe of profit; nor till they were wholly undone did they difcover, and then by the perception of feeling only, that Five was lefs than Nine.

Gentlemen will obferve, that this calculation in their paper goes no farther than Chriftmas, 1771. The two fubfequent years 1772 and 1773 will afford fome peculiar obfervations, which I hope may throw fome commercial lights into the Committee; lights I hope intelligible without commercial practice. Will gentlemen pleafe to look over the

D   paper

paper. (No. 12) they will find in the years 1770 and 1771, the increase of Linen imported was very confiderable; fo they will find the cafe of Linen and all other articles, either home-made or imported, that could fupply the North American markets. The expectation of an immenfe export to that country upon their cancelling their non-importation contract, naturally produced this increafe of ftock in all kinds of goods, foreign or home-made, for that market. Unfortunately, Sir, at this very crifis, the pernicious paper circulation was in full action, and by the creation of falfe capitals encouraged fo many adventurers to engage in this export, that the American markets became over ftocked; and what was in itfelf an advantage became a difafter. Thus, Sir, I do not allow, that even the over-ftocking the American markets was a caufe even in concurrence of the calamities I began with defcribing; it was itfelf an effect of the original, primary caufe, the paper circulation: but the difafter was not known in time to prevent more mifchief in 1772; for,

Sir,

Sir, the Irish in that fatal year furnished a very full quantity, twenty millions and a half of yards, the Scotch above thirteen millions; a trifle less than in 1771; the foreign merchants twenty-seven millions, about a million less than the year before; a quantity upon the whole too large for any usual demand. In this state intelligence was received, that goods sold to loss in North America. Upon this, Sir, the grand northern apparatus of the philosopher's stone was overset; and all that stagnation, all these evils ensued: the merchant and manufacturer were found loaded with goods, which they could not sell. This, Sir, is a natural effect of the original cause. Then, Sir, a monitor more powerful than King, Lords and Commons, or all the powers upon earth, the irresistible monitor, necessity, took place of prudence. What was the consequence in 1773? The Irish in 1773 reduced their quantity only about two millions of yards, one tenth part; the Scotch, *pro hac vice* wiser than the Irish, reduced theirs from thirteen millions to ten millions seven hundred thou-

sand

sand yards. The merchant, rather more en-
lightened, and endued with more forecaft than
the manufacturer, reduced his from twenty-
feven millions to feventeen and a half, the
loweft import that ever was known : and in
that very year, the authors of all the mifchief
accufed the merchants of having brought over
fuch a quantity of Linen, as occafioned all
their diftrefs. This is the ftate of the cafe.
Thus, Sir, I have fhewn, what was the real
caufe of the evil in the firft inftance, and in
this laft what was not, if there is any truth in
figures. Here I muft obferve, low as the
import of foreign Linen was in the year 1773,
when it was accufed of an increafe, it will ftill
be lower this year. I do not fpeak merely
from the opinion, either of Mr. Milloway or
my own, or the Hamburgh merchants put
together; I have really enquired, and find by
the Ship Brokers, that the Hamburgh merchants this fpring have brought one third lefs
than they brought at this time laft year;
a fortunate event to one kingdom, an inno-
cent partaker of the mifchiefs refulting from
the

the projects of the other; fortunate too for
that laſt, if at length, warned by their own
ſelf-created ſufferings, they will learn to controul that inordinate and intemperate ambition, which, deſpiſing advantages ſlow
but ſure, and forcing births premature,
hath produced ſo many ruinous abortions.
They are moſt of them ſcholars.; they will
find that ſentiment better expreſſed in the original, the wiſeſt of Roman hiſtorians, under
the head of Brutidius Niger, in theſe words de-
ſcribing Men, *Qui, ſpretis, quæ tarda cum ſecuri-
tate, præmatura vel cum exitio properant**. I
would likewiſe recommend the whole paſſage
to their ſerious attention, as a preparation for
their only remedy, far different from any they
have yet ſuggeſted for themſelves. This
brings me to that part, where I am to conſider,
what are not the remedies. And here, Sir, I
take the moſt open ground of an advocate, the
friendlieſt of advocates of our home manufacture of linen, in particular the Scotch; as a
partiality is due to a country the deepeſt in
diſtreſs: but, Sir, ſevere ſincerity is a part of
friendſhip,

* Tacit, Ann. 3, C. 66.

friendfhip, nay force to hold back the hand of error from diftempered lips, eager to fwallow poifon for a medicine. I think, Sir, now, whatever may have been the projects at firft intended, or now meditated, or even wifhed for on this fubject, I fay, after having ftudied it for forty years; and courting fuch an occafion as this, I am determined, if you will condefcend to hear me, that the whole and every part of this important queftion fhall be fifted to the bottom once for all. Sir, the firft idea, but I call it project—I will prove all to be project.—the firft project is an impofition (we talk from public notoriety, not from matter of fuppofition) of ten per cent. upon all foreign linen imported. I aver, that upon the ten fpecies of narrow German linen, the duty for many years paft is about 27 per cent. upon the prime coft, computed to the time the goods are put on board the fhips for London ; but minute calculators may add forty fhillings more for the freight and infurance to London, which will make twenty-feven upon one hundred and two. As for my own imports, I
folemnly

folemnly declare upon the niceft calculation for years back, I pay more than thirty per cent. I pay thirty per cent. but there is a reafon ; I deal more in the lower fort. I ftated about twenty-feven, as the medium price upon all German linen imported. I have proved by that moft candid and weighty witnefs Mr. Pearfon, that under the old duties foreign linens, and fome of the bulkieft, are run into feveral parts of England. When I mention my own imports paying thirty per cent. thefe new calculators tell me I pay but fifteen, according to their mode of computing duties in their country. If they were to tell me they did not pay a fhilling, I would not difpute their veracity. I beg they would not difpute mine. I did allude to an afperfion thrown out, (I, it is true have proved a clandeftine import into England) but as to the afperfions, which have been thrown out, that even the merchants themfelves are guilty of abufes in the entries, I fhall only remind the calculators for the prefent of an old Spanifh proverb,---He whofe houfe is made of glafs, fhould not be the firft to throw ftones.

ftones. I have defcribed a certain national propehfity in one region to projects ; there is another propenfity, which the very fight, air and fmell of the fea ftimulates immediately to action. Sir, that propenfity is fo ftrong and fo prevalent, that the greateft public undertaking there was abufed to the encouragement of that propenfity, under the fpecious title of promoting agriculture, trade and manufactures. The firft and nobleft in dignity and fortune, diftinguifhed more for their honour and probity, than for their rank and titles, were deluded and deceived*. And numbers of

men

* And grofsly injured, might be added. Every Man of common fenfibility and rectitude, muft have felt the ftrongeft indignation to have feen fo much virtue made the property of clandeftine artifice. A bill of pains and penalties was applied in 1720. With equal juftice the fame rigid meafure is applicable to 1772, an æra more fatal than the former, to the trade and manufactures of thefe kingdoms. Let it be obferved, however, that the general ftagnation was owing to a numerous train of other defeated projectors, who fhall be namelefs, and was more apprehended, than derived from Meffrs. Douglas, Heron and Co. The higheft acknowledgments and veneration are due from the whole community, to the illuftrious and

wo, thy

men have felt to their coſt, that that ſociety, the greateſt ever formed without a charter, which at one time could iſſue eight hundred thouſand pounds in paper, and drain the city of London of ſix hundred thouſand pounds in hard money, was originally, who can diſpute it, the device of ſmugglers; and by their influence in the direction, capitals were furniſhed to noted ſmuggling ſocieties to the amount of twenty-eight thouſand pounds in one inſtance the moſt notorious of all. I do not mention this by way of retaliation; but I mention it as argument. This inference may be drawn from the practice of both kingdoms, that at any time, from any quarter, where this propenſity prevails the moſt, any propoſition for an increaſe of duty, already heavy, ſhould be received by the Legiſlature with a jealous ear. Here I ſtep forth again in behalf of the honeſt Scotch manufacturer. He, Sir, not ſpeculating beyond his loom, taking

E   all

worthy part of that unfortunate ſociety, who at ſo exorbitant an expence to themſelves, did not leave a ſingle bill of theirs unpaid.

all for encouragement which comes from Parliament, particularly this addition of Ten per cent. upon twenty-seven, will double his Induſtry, will over-ſtock himſelf, and find himſelf after all his labour ſupplanted by the ſmuggler. I do not deal in aſſertion: I reſt upon a faƈt, proved at your Bar. When the cambricks were put under a prohibition, two manufaƈtures were ſoon eſtabliſhed; one in the South, which loſt all their capital, I fancy more; the other in the North: they, Sir, were great ſufferers; becauſe the ſmugglers ſupplied all the markets in England.

The next projeƈt is to retain the new duty upon export to the Colonies. Two conſequences may be clearly foreſeen; the poor induſtrious Scotchman will exert himſelf again under the double deluſion of a ſuppoſed encouragement, and at firſt the ſudden vent of his goods; for I know, Sir, that in caſe it were poſſible this could paſs, there are adventurers in that country, who would immediately have another ſecond ſight of great acquiſitions from the American markets; would ſhip large cargoes of linen, taken up upon

credit,

credit ; they would get thither, and find the market poffeffed by the clandeftine import of foreign Linen. Sir, I repeat again, it is forty years I have been ferioufly confidering the merits of this affair, and frequently in con-junction with my brethren have oppofed, par-ticularly, the difallowance of drawback upon exportation. The whole body of Plantation merchants always joined in the oppofition upon a fact, from time immemorial, that fo-reign Linens were run into thofe parts. It is true, Sir, that there have been well-difpofed Colonifts, who ufed confiderable quantities of linen through the channel of the Mother-country, though they could have had them Twenty per cent. at leaft cheaper directly from the foreigner ; and now, Sir, when there is fcarce a well-difpofed Colonift left, when they have been exerting the moft contumacious and ferocious difobedience on account of one tax, it is fuggefted to impofe another ; as if linen could not be run into America with the fame facility as tea, or as a pipe of wine into Great-Britain. By this means you are really raifing an encouragement to their fmugglers from

E 2   Twenty

Twenty to Thirty per cent; twenty per
cent. it cofts already to go through the Mother-
country to America; and on the head of emigration, admitting all are weavers, you would
be virtually giving a bounty to the diligence
and fkill of thofe new fettlers, to rival you
there in the Linen manufacture of this country. In the mean time, what becomes of your
adventurer? His goods will remain unfold,
I mean the adventurer who fent out Scotch
linen upon credit: no return will come home;
he will become infolvent, and the poor, injured, deluded manufacturer may make frefh
application for relief to you, to you for ever molefted with applications to atchieve impoffibili-
ties: as if an Act of Parliament could regulate
the conduct of a projector, in defpite of his
folly, or allot to every acre of land a fpe-
cific produce in defiance of the feafon.
But the other ill confequence of a more formidable nature, my honourable hearers may
find in the printed report, (N°. 17) the gra-
dual increafe of the linens exported from the
Scotch and Irifh manufacturers to North
America, under the head of what bounties
have been received; add to this the linens,
which

which are exported without bounty. I will venture to call the whole together at above four hundred thoufand pounds a year, of which the better half falls to the fhare of Scotland. I am almoft difpofed to quote Tacitus again ; would thefe people leave fuch a value at the mercy of American fmugglers ; if they do, I believe it will be loft; and then I do not want to be affured, that nothing more is wanting to compleat the mifery and defolation of their country : and thus by the impofition of new duties at home, and the retention of them, upon exportation, Parliament will run the rifk of ftrangling the manufacture, the fmuggler of America holding one end of the cord, and the fmuggler of Great Britain the other.

I am now come to that part of the fubject, which with fubmiffion I believe, you will deem of moft confequence. I addrefs you in your mixt capacity of fenators and ftatefmen. I name the revolution ; an æra which all muft hear with reverence; an æra, which not only eftablifhed your civil and religious rights at home, but provided for them an impregnable

bulwark

bulwark againſt foreign attacks by eſtabliſh-
ing your ſyſtem of foreign trade. Throw
back your reflection upon the glorious annals
of your country from your deliverers firſt war
with France down to the laſt. What fortunate means have enabled this iſland to endure
a drain of more than one hundred millions during a period of about ſeventy years? The
ſupreme guardian of all, among the multitude
of his bleſſings on this iſland, has rendered its
ſoil unfruitful in precious metals ; he hath
given you materials to exerciſe the faculties
imparted to your people, endurance of labour,
induſtry and ſkill. Parliament, as far as hu-
man perfection can extend, have adopted and
purſued this great and original plan. By their
prudent interpoſition, new materials have been
borrowed from foreigners, diverſity of new
produce, raiſed in diſtant ſettlements for the
further exertion of your national activity, in-
vention and toil; which applied by the merchant, have formed that vaſt and multifarious
machine, that ſublime ſyſtem of foreign trade,
whence your arts and induſtry have derived
ſuch an influx of wealth, as hath ſupported a
ſucceſſion

fucceffion of expenfive wars, unmatched in
hiftory, and leaves you ftill in rank, among
the firft of nations. Would the finger of policy touch the fmalleft part of fuch a fyftem
but with a trembling delicacy ? Yet now the
boifterous hand of project is ftretched forth to
fhatter the whole frame.

Sir, I muft now trouble you with a little
more calculation. Upon this head, I muft
begin by removing fome fmall obftructions
thrown in my Way. You have a paper, Sir,
I think in the report, which ftates the exports
to Germany and the exports to Ireland : I
may add that the exports to Scotland, the export from the city of London to every fea-
port, market town and village in England,
would have made the value a great deal higher, and would have furnifhed matter for my
new calculators to exercife their faculties upon.
Are not the Englifh, Scotch and Irifh all fel-
low fubjects under the fame head ; and were
they altogether unconnected with the reft of
the globe, would there not be a great traffic
carried on amongft themfelves, and the community not one fhilling richer or poorer ? I
wifh

wifh the other two kingdoms took lefs from England, and fpent lefs in it, upon the principle, that no great members can decay without prejudice to the whole, as England has found to her coft. Traffic therefore between fubject and fubject cannot be productive of any national wealth. Sir, there can be no propofition more felf-evident, than that, fo far as every part of a great community throws produce and manufactures into the foreigner's markets, fo far as he takes from you more, than you take from him, in that proportion, and by thefe means only can you receive wealth. It is by thefe means you have increafed to fuch a degree, as to render you fecure at home, and formidable to your enemies. Sir, it is certain that you muft fupply your wants from other places, not merely, Sir, for your manufactures ; there is a material you want for your prefervation and your very being ; or you would not have a fhip of war, or a merchantman. Firft let us change the laws of nature, and then tell foreign nations, you will raife every article within your-
.felves;

felves for your own ufe, and they fhall take
every article from us for their ufe. ·

. Sir, I have fhewn, that by retaining drawbacks you hazard a lofs of four hundred thoufand pounds a year in linen vended to America.
Suppofe, Sir, that by the impofition of new
duties at home, you fhould fucceed, that you
fhould at once annihilate the ufe and confumption of all German and Dutch linens,
and by a miracle, your home manufacture
fhould inftantly fupply the confumers wants
in cheapnefs, quantity and quality ; what will
be your object ? You have a paper upon your
table which gives you the medium value for
ten years of Dutch and German linen imported, about four hundred and feventy thoufand
pounds a year. I cannot allow all that as
gain ; I muft deduct one hundred and feventy
thoufand pounds for the foreign yarn, which
is notoriously ufed in the Britifh fabrick, for
which I refer gentlemen to the Paper
(N° 14) which fhews the great increafe of foreign yarn imported : therefore all the poffible
object of advantage may be fet at three hundred
thoufand pounds upon an hypotbefis in itfelf
F impoffible.

impoffible. Now let us confider on the other hand what you put in hazard. . Mr. Payne has given you a ftate of your exports in two periods of five years each, in one from 1762 to 1766, the annual medium is about 4,000,000; in the fecond period from 1767 to 1771, the annual medium is reduced to 3,000,000. It is ftill an immenfe object. I muft now remove another objection :- I may be told the cuftom-houfe ftate of thefe exports is vague; granted, Sir; I will allow 500,000l. for errors; this leaves a remainder of 2,000,000 and a half; ftill an immenfe object. But, Sir, I certainly of all men muft grant, that thefe cuf-tom-houfe accounts are vague. When I had the honour of a feat within the bar, I was the firft for many years, who called for thofe ac- counts. I had many conferences with the of- ficers. I know their mode is vague, I know they go upon the fame plan, as fince the firft inftitution of the infpector's office by the ad- vice of Dr. Davenant. What is the inference? To carry their point, your new calculators, never looking upon both fides of a queftion, fay, the infpector has over-valued your ex- ports;

ports; when I reply, they are under-valued,
I do not mean to set one affertion againft the
other. I will fupport mine, at leaft by pro-
bable conjecture. I take the reduced ftate of
the exports at 3,000,000. I deduct 1,100,000*l*.
the total import from Germany and Holland;
there remains a balance of 1,900,000*l*. If
there is no more, we are in a deplorable ftate.
Now I beg you will honour me with fome attention. I believe, Sir, every one of my
honourable hearers will allow, if we owe any
debt to Holland and Germany on any other
account, part of our balance in trade will be
applied to difcharge that debt. I don't know
whether any gentleman remembers, that I did
ftate it in 1763, when within the bar. Sir,
you pay to thofe countries, particularly Holland, to a day about 900,000*l*. for the divi-
dend on their fhare in your funds; that muft
be paid by part of the balance they owe to you
on trade. Another thing will be allowed to
be very obvious too; if we owe a balance of
trade to thofe countries, which border upon
Holland and Germany, where this balance is
due to us, it will naturally centre in Ham-

burg

burgh, but in Amſterdam chiefly, whence by
negociation of exchange it will be applied to
diſcharge that balance. I don't pretend to be
accurate, *Valeat quantum valere poteſt.* We
certainly do pay to Sweden, Norway, Ruſſia,
and the Eaſt country above a million a year for
materials, without which you could not ſub-
ſiſt. There are other incidents, many things
I have not mentioned. I have taken up too
much of your time already. I have a great
deal more to ſay. Now, Sir, I will give another conjecture. In 1771 the export of Britiſh
produce and manufactures together to Germany is ſet down at three hundred and eighty-
ſix thouſand pounds, and for the five years
of that laſt period, at a medium, the
whole value of Britiſh produce and manufactures comes to about half a million a year.
I have a paper, I believe, more accurate; it is
a paper authentic, and being right in one article out of four, gives credit to the other
three. It gives a ſtate of the export of Saxon
linen to England, and of three only of our
manufactures into that country. They give
you the value of their linen at one hundred
and

and fixty-fix thoufand pounds, which we will
admit to be a very juft valuation. Sir, the value of our hardware, furriery, and woollen goods
is three hundred and forty thoufand pounds.
Gentlemen, remember Mr. Rafch's evidence:
if Saxony in three articles only takes off three
hundred and forty thoufand pounds, and
under this head produce is not to be reckoned,
I fubmit, whether one hundred and fixty
thoufand pounds a year is not too little for the
fupply direct of all Germany befides. The
Cuftom-Houfe accounts put them in only at
half a million. I think it is impoffible, but
that they do undervalue the manufactures of
this country: I could fay, our own manufacturers and exporters are of the fame opinion ;
however, I will take no advantage of thefe
conjectures: I will revert to the reduced ftate
of the exports at three millions; only obferv-
ing that four fifths of thofe to Holland go
from thence to Germany. Now, Sir, fhall
that be expofed to any degree of refentment
from foreign Princes ? For what ? For pro-
curing an opportunity for your manufacturers
to try an experiment, which may not fucceed
perhaps

perhaps in half a century, and certainly hath hitherto made fo little progrefs in the linens confumed by our poor againft the German under the prefent duty of 27 per cent. To gain what? Why, no more than three hundred thoufand pounds a year. In the mean time all the poor of England, the labourer, mechanic, and manufacturer, muft be taxed Ten per cent. for all they ufe: they cannot bear that tax: they muft be paid more for their labour, and the tax muft be diffufed all over England. Hence you are expofing your own manufactures to gain yearly three hundred thoufand pounds only; whilft in the mean time you tax the country in this cruel manner. I always make a referve: the fmuggler is always very ready to give relief: he may relieve. Now, Sir, having confidered the projects of the upper clafs, I will defcend to thofe of the loweft, which I muft beg leave to call the fediment of the crucible. I do flatter myfelf the great apparatus will be overfet; there may be fome hopes the rate of Silefia linens may be raifed, being that fort which certainly exceeds eight-pence an ell;

there

there may be some expectation that at least we may raise the rate upon that, notwithstanding the rate now at a medium of all the narrow German linen is as much as can be, being rather more than prime cost. Upon this head I shall be very short: You have heard Mr. Rasch. I beg leave to recommend every one of my honorable hearers to look over any common map of Germany, and if he can find any one Potentate, who commands the channels of communication in Germany, thro' which three or four millions a year must go; if he can find out who is master of the Vistula; who is master of the Oder, by Stetin; who is master of the Elbe where Hamburgh lies; and through whose dominions that river runs; who is master of the Weser by Minden, where Bremen stands; who is master of the Embs by Embden, and of the Rhine by Wesel; you will find that your whole export which goes through Germany, (the greatest part I allow for the consumption there) but which actually reaches Poland, Alsace, and Loraine, &c. (there is likewise a very great value goes to France through Germany) I

say

fay you will expofe all this to the mercy of
that Potentate, who commands the whole,
and who would be lefs offended at your laying
a general impofition upon all linens, than
fetting a ftigma upon his in particular. It is
fo evident in point of policy, I will not trouble
the Committee with any thing more upon that
head. However, Sir, there is another very
minute project indeed, and of all others the
moft inconfiftent with Englifh generofity and
juftice, the putting the Silefia damafks and
tabling upon the footing of the Holland
bleach, which has been proved to you will
amount to a prohibition. It has been proved
to you that thefe linens are made in Saxony, a
friendly power. The ftate of your trade in
his country I have already produced : your
goods pay but a tranfit of about Two per
cent. add to this the excife paid by his fubjects
for thofe confumed at home; they amount
together but to a trifle more than half of what
his linens pay here. What we pay him for
thefe articles does not exceed 20,000 l. a Year.
Is it poffible, a Britifh Parliament can treat a
friend fo. I muft now make ufe of my main
argument.

Argument. I am ferious, when I talk in the manner I am going to do. I am a friend of the Scotch manufacturer. I have in my eye again that deluded man, who would go to work to make damafks and diapers; he will find himfelf fupplanted by the fmugglers again. I fay every lady has as good a right to cover her table with fmuggled damafks, as her hufband has to fet on his fmuggled wine. Will the opulent be reftrained in their luxury? I have drank fmuggled wine at the table of a Firft Commiffioner of the Treafury: I have told him fo; had not his wife a right to cover it with fmuggled damafk? Why, Sir, if every mafter of a family were as rigid as Cato the Cenfor, he could only anfwer for himfelf; he could not reftrain the female part of his family in their dear delight of purchafing pennyworths from fmugglers. Sir, the laft remains of our broken crucible is the difallowance of the drawbacks upon foreign Linen printed here. I believe the evidence of Mr. Walker cannot be well forgot. The export is very confiderable; his alone 50,000 *l.* a year: the value of the labour, induftry, and fkill, ex-

G   ceeds

ceeds the value of the material. We give no offence to Germany by this; she will thank us for it, being an encouragement for her numerous manufactures in printed linen, to expel you from every market in Europe and its Colonies. I shall close this head with a reference once more to Mr. Payne's state of exports for the two periods, and shall add a dissection and corollary of my own, which fills me with very alarming ideas. Sir, of the five millions (gentlemen, I believe, remember, the first period produced four millions a year, and the last three) of the five millions lost in the last period, four millions fall on your manufactures. First I must premise; in the Custom-house accounts you see two heads of exports; one under foreign goods and merchandise, the other under British manufactures and produce. The decrease on the foreign part is but *eight hundred and fifty thousand pounds*, the remaining *four millions, one hundred and sixty thousand* consist of British manufactures and produce*.

Sir,

---
* To satisfy the curious, the annual mediums of British manufacture and produce, exported to Holland and Germany,

Sir, the produce cannot amount to more.
than the odd money ; the produce being lead,
falt, coal, tin and other trifling articles ; therefore the remaining decrease of four millions
falls upon your manufacture at the rate of
eight hundred thousand pounds a year. Now,
Sir, I have got to compare with this decreafe
a ftate to fhew, whether in the fame period the
Linen manufacture has decreafed in proportion. Sir, upon their own paper, and upon
their own value I find, while your exports decreafed in that proportion, which fell upon your
manufactures, principally the woollen, that
the linen manufacture has increafed above
three hundred thoufand pounds a year ; what
are we to underftand by all thefe complaints ?
I defire to know, what check have they met
with ? Sir, it appears by thofe papers, that

many, are here fubjoined, for four periods of five Years
each, inftead of the two above :

1752 to 1756 inclufive, about 1,622,000.
1757   1761   1,800,000.
1762   1766   2,040,000.
1767   1771   1,216,000.

1772 and 1773, at a medium, 1,031,000.

they

they have increased above three hundred thoufand pounds a year, while your manufacturers
decreased eight hundred thoufand pounds a
year. Here, Sir, I defire to hear no more of
the vague accounts of the Cuftom-houfe, but
inftead of 4,000,000 call the firft, four parts;
inftead of 3,000,000 call the laft, three parts:
then I tell thofe, who did not upon one occafion know, that Five was lefs than Nine, and
on another that Twenty-five was lefs than
Thirty, I do infift upon it that Three is lefs
than Four; in that proportion have your exports decreafed. No doubt, there are errors
in the Cuftom-houfe accounts; but as thofe
errors are common to all periods, the proportion of increafe and decreafe is true. If four
be more than three, which is my way of cal-
culating, there is a decreafe of one fourth part;
of that, four fifths fall upon your manufactures.
I will tell another moft extraordinary thing: of
that decreafe in your manufactures near three
fourths is in the export to Germany, and but
little more than one fourth to Holland, though
Holland for twenty years together hath taken
                              confiderably

considerably more of your exports than Germany; but the exports direct to Germany chiefly go to that part where their linen fabricks are
carried on. I muft mention an æra that appears very fingular to me, others may call it
ominous. The year I look back to is 1767,
when I had the honour of a feat among you, I
did with others oppofe a new duty upon German linen, upon the fame principles and arguments I ufed this day; a predominant intereft
over-powered us : but it is ftrange, that the
decline in your woollen manufacture juft
coincided with that year, in which you laid the
new duties particularly upon Silefia lawns.
This beng the cafe, your linens increafed, as
your woollens decreafed ; and this all proved
from their own papers. I have in the begin-
ning of my difcourfe, Sir, admitted a decline ;
fo I did. What is the nature of that decline
and the extent of it, I will explain to you.
There was no other check, but what came
from the paper circulation ; I know of no
other. Your exports plainly have been
checked. What is the nature of that check
upon

upon the linens ? They made the full quantity, in 1772; in 1773 Ireland made a tenth part lefs than they did the year before; which, Sir, is a fluctuation, that may be the effect of any common cafualty in any great manufacture; and to fay becaufe in 1773 they made two millions two hundred thoufand yards lefs than in 1772, that, that has occafioned an emigration of 30,000 people.—Sir, it is an affront to your underftanding to come and alledge fuch an argument as this. Such an accident might have happened without any man's being able to affign any caufe at all. Whim, fancy, mode will make an alteration of a tenth part one year with another. Add the Scotch and Irifh together, it is but a feventh or eighth part diminution in both, between 1772 and 1773 : it is all the check they have met with from that paper circulation, which fhook the credit of England to its bafis. Why now, Sir, let us add, that in 1773 foreign linen was reduced a third ; in 1774 I pledge myfelf it will be reduced lower. As thefe people have the markets here before them, and their

their ancient competitor in this crippled
ftate, with what propriety, with what deco-
rum is any favour of any fort due to them;
who have been proved to be increafing, when
your great ftaple was decreafing, and is ftill
from no other caufe, but from the dreadful
northern projects ; while the linens are now in
a fituation to be envied by every other manufacture, even by that great ftaple itfelf. Sir,
afking a favour under thefe circumftances for
a manufacture, is over-looking your own great
ftaple. Sir, fuch a preference would be an
infult upon the firft intereft of this country,
the landed intereft ; it would be an infult upon
the fecond, the commercial and manufacturing
intereft ; it would be an infult upon the common fenfe of every rank and order in this
country. And why ? Sir, is it becaufe your
own manufacturers have not vexed Parliament
with applications, have not applied to you,
Sir, as the grand phyfician of the ftate, and
treated you, as an empiric to undertake dif-
tempers incurable, but by time and neceffity ?
Is it becaufe their complaints have been only
                                        whifpered,

whifpered and murmured within their own neighbourhood? Have you not feen the ftreets of the capital filled with mendicant cries of miferable fwarms from the filk manufactory? Were not thefe people content to render themfelves the objects of private charity? Did they come to your door? Who is it that has molefted Parliament and exhaufted your time? Did other manufacturers, particularly the poor Weavers, under all the horrors of northern paper circulation, which even diminifhed the traffick and confumption among yourfelves? Did they not fubmit in quiet, did they afk your aid? No, Sir, they never wearied and troubled Parliament? Is Parliament, are committees to fit, is the whole Houfe to be taken up under all thefe circumftances, which I do fay, I have proved? Is it for one manufacture, in a ftate to be envied at this time by your woollen manufactures? As if the firft in that envied ftate are the only objects of parliamentary attention; and muft you overlook all others, becaufe they have been filent, becaufe they have been patient, while thofe

others,

others, Sir, the authors of all the evils (I say
again) defperate in undertakings, even of credulity and hope; defperate alike under difap-
pointments, whether imaginary or real, are
now come not intentionally, but eventually
to widen the wound already given to your own
great ftaple, to empty your populous towns
by unravelling, with obtufe and impolitic
violence, a texture woven with fo much attention by the wifdom of your fathers, and main-
tained by your own ; that texture, which the
guardian power of your ifland extends over
the whole empire, to diftribute thofe copious
faculties, which conftitute your national fecu-
rity and greatnefs, I mean your fyftem of foreign trade : And upon what allegations, upon what calculations, what arguments and deductions I need not repeat. And what time
has this unfortunate people chofen to raife a
flame among all the great interefts of this
country ? At a time, I tell them, when the
falvation of their country depends upon the
faculties of England, and her liberal and immediate application of them to preferve a reft-

H   lefs,

lefs, ambitious and improvident fifter. Sir, this leads me now to the laft head of my fubject. I have fhewn you not only the caufe of the diftemper, but where it lies : Sir, it lies there ftill; that fifter is as much diftempered as ever, and fhe muft be faved ; for it is impoffible that Scotland can fall, but London muft totter: and yet, Sir, her diftemper is of fo peculiar a fort, that it is not curable by time and neceffity ; but it may by Parliament. Now, Sir, I will fhew to you what the diforder is. In confequence of fo many unfuccefsful projects (I fhall not be contradicted, Sir,) fhe has contracted a capital of debt to England, a recent debt, all within four years, which fhe can't pay; it would be injurious and indecent for me to hint at any thing more than one fociety, about which I profeffed never to keep a fecret; it now owes 600,000*l.* Pay-day muft come ; I hint at nothing elfe. Payments in the fhape of intereft and annuities have created an annual drain upon that country it cannot bear. There is another new annual drain created by their own credulity, which taking their increafed paper currency for an addition

of

[51]

of folid wealth, increafed their expence of living in proportion : The imaginary wealth is vanifhed, and the habit of expence remains. I do take upon me to fay, I defy all Scotland to fay, they underftand their affairs, as well as I do ; no, Sir, not all Scotland together. I don't fpeak with vanity, I pay myfelf no compliment, when I fay fo. Then Sir, what muft be done ? Nothing, but an immediate influx of money. England I believe is awakened from her ftupefaction, and will no longer be fafcinated at the fight of Scotch acceptances and indorfements. Money they have not. Now I come with my remedy. You have already paffed one bill to ratify the agreements made with the annuitants of Douglas, Heron and Co. Sir, I make no doubt, you paffed that bill upon thofe principles correfponding with your dignity, which are publick principles ; if that propofal had not taken place, you would have feen the fame fcene of defolation in 1774 as in 1772, therefore it was from publick principles. The authors of that bill acted upon thofe principles, to protect publick credit from

H 2   fuch

such another stunning blow, which it received in 1772. All is due to the noble personages in that affair; whom I not only love and esteem, but admire ; they by the severest losses purchased an opportunity of shewing to God and man, how much the chaste light of honour and probity exceeded the glare of pomp and title. ⊥ But their own in this affair was but a secondary consideration. I have taken up too much of your time already, or I could demonstrate from facts, taken upon my own knowledge, that you would have seen a return of the same desolation before the expiration of 1774. This is only a part of a plan to save Scotland. I believe, we shall not lend them money on their bills and notes ; but are willing to lend them money upon land, an indubitable security incapable of fallacy. I cannot miss this opportunity of recommending another Bill, which is under the consideration of the learned Gentlemen of both kingdoms. I am so convinced of the necessity of it ; I cannot omit this opportunity of recommending what I mean by a radical cure. There are objections to Scotch mortgages, which

will

will deter English lenders. In the first place,
money lent upon a Scotch mortgage is not
personal property, nor deviseable by will:
John Bull will not lend upon such principles;
and if you want the principal, it is not re-
coverable as in England. Sir, there must be
a bill, which is under consideration, to put
Scotch mortgages upon the footing of English
ones. Now, Sir, it will be an advantage to
the South-Briton to lend out his money, so
perfectly secure upon so high an Interest. It
will be in the power of the North-Briton to
pay that interest, from the profitable use he
will make of the money; for by that means,
in a few years, he may be enabled to pay his
debts, and to be at ease, like the other parts
of the kingdom: and this, Sir, will tend to
extract the very root of all their distemper,
which is pride and ambition, upon this
axiom, that in all communities which are most
at their ease, the spirit of project prevails the
least. I want to put Scotland into that state
of ease: they then would find, how much
more comfortable it is to enjoy advantages

flow and fure, from moderate, temperate trade, and look back with horror upon thofe paroxyfms of mind in that dreadful interval between the birth of a project, and its laft fatal diffolution. They have room for improvements; they can make ten, fifteen, twenty per cent. and afford to pay you five: you by thefe means make a fifter kingdom happy, and cure her both in mind and body.

Now, Sir, my peroration fhall confift in a fingle requeft, that you, Sir, and the Committee will be pleafed to accept fuch expreffions, my gratitude may furnifh, of fenfibility for fo much indulgence, fo much of your time and patience; and if, Sir, I have performed what I undertook; if I have afcertained the genuine caufe of the diforder; if I have fhewn what are not the remedies, what is the nature of the diftemper, and what is the cure: if, Sir, I have ufed no language illiberal, no argument fallacious, no allegation untrue; if, Sir, befides the accuftomed grace and humanity within thefe walls to all, who appear open and undifguifed at the Bar; if befides the

complacency

complacency of thofe among my honourable hearers, who may not know me, or the partiality of thofe who do, I may, Sir, be difmiffed from this place, under the humble hope of having obtained the fmalleft fhare of your folid approbation, in confequence of having thrown the flighteft fpark of light upon a fubject fo copious and national, this laborious exertion of mine, full late in life, and I truft the laft, will be deemed by me as aufpicious and honourable for the remainder of my days.

APPENDIX.

APPENDIX.

NUMBER XII.

Total Quantities of Foreign LINENS imported into England from Christmas 1751 to Christmas 1771.

	Yards.
1752	27,856,122 $\frac{3}{4}$
1753	35,372,907
1754	39,871,973 $\frac{1}{2}$
1755	31,947,447
1756	31,759,234 $\frac{1}{4}$
1757	28,429,072 $\frac{1}{2}$
1758	29,770,104 $\frac{1}{4}$
1759	25,057,533 $\frac{1}{2}$
1760	27,988,972 $\frac{1}{4}$
1761	30,428,424

Yards.

299,481,791 $\frac{1}{4}$ Tot. which is 29,948,179 *per An.*

1762	18,827,853 $\frac{1}{4}$
1763	26,634,851
1764	28,092,215 $\frac{1}{4}$
1765	25,497,795 $\frac{1}{4}$
1766	25,624,107 $\frac{1}{2}$
1767	21,054,411
1768	23,112,349
1769	25,431,162 $\frac{1}{4}$
1770	27,101,343 $\frac{1}{4}$
1771	28,243,121 $\frac{1}{4}$

Yards.

249,619,210 $\frac{1}{2}$ Tot. which is 24,961,921 *per An.*

1772	27,338,881
1773	17,725,443

Total Quantities of Foreign LINENS exported from England from Chriftmas 1751 to Chriftmas 1773.

Yards.

1752	7,187,110½
1753	7,448,672¼
1754	6,981,528¾
1755	7,542,694¼
1756	8,461,726
1757	8,461,031½
1758	7,989,160
1759	10,482,730¼
1760	10,079,851½
1761	6,740,960½

Yards.

81,375,466¼ Total; which is 8,137,546 per An.

1762	5,990,706½
1763	8,046,855¼
1764	7,889,265¼
1765	6,394,147
1766	7,171,891
1767	7,174,784
1768	8,046,980¼
1769	7,102,527¼
1770	8,461,546¼
1771	10,470,129½

76,748,833¼ Total; which is 7,674,883 per An.

| 1772 | | 8,721,791 |
| 1773 | | 7,058,921 |

I   Total

Total Quantities of Irish LINENS exported from Ireland from March 25, 1751, to March 25, 1773, as delivered by Mr. *Henry Betty.*

	Yards.
1752	10,656,003
1753	10,493,858
1754	12,092,487 ¼
1755	13,379,733 ½
1756	13,272,884 ½
1757	15,508,709
1758	14,982,557 ¼
1759	14,093,431
1760	13,375,456 ¼
1761	12,048,881 ½

129,904,001 ½ Tot. which is 12,990,400 *per An.*

1762	15,559,676
1763	16,013,105 ¼
1764	15,101,081 ¾
1765	14,355,205
1766	17,892,102 ¼
1767	20,148,170 ¼
1768	18,490,019 ½
1769	17,790,705
1770	20,560,754
1771	25,376,808

181,287,627 Tot. which is 18,128,762 ½ *per An.*

1772	20,599,178 ½
1773	18,450,700 ½

Total

Total Quantities of Scotch LINENS, stamped for Sale in Scotland from the 1st of Nov. 1751 to the 1st of Nov. 1773, as delivered by Mr. *George Goldie.*

	Yards.
1752	8,759,943 $\frac{1}{8}$
1753	9,422,593 $\frac{6}{8}$
1754	8,914,369
1755	8,122,472 $\frac{1}{8}$
1756	8,547,153 $\frac{5}{8}$
1757	9,764,408 $\frac{7}{8}$
1758	10,624,435 $\frac{5}{8}$
1759	10,830,707
1760	11,747,728 $\frac{6}{8}$
1761	11,995,494

Yards.

98,729,306 $\frac{1}{8}$ Tot. which is 9,872,930 $\frac{4}{8}$ per An.

1762	11,303,237
1763	12,399,656 $\frac{4}{8}$
1764	12,823,048 $\frac{1}{8}$
1765	12,746,659 $\frac{4}{8}$
1766	13,224,557
1767	12,783,043
1768	11,795,437
1769	13,406,125
1770	13,049,535
1771	13,466,274 $\frac{4}{8}$

126,997,572 $\frac{1}{8}$ Tot. which is 12,699,757 $\frac{3}{8}$ per An.

| 1772 | 13,089,006 $\frac{1}{2}$ |
| 1773 | 10,748,110 $\frac{1}{2}$ |

I 2   Total

Total Quantities of Irish L I N E N S, imported into England from Chriftmas 1756
to Chriftmas 1773.

	Yards.
1757	11,925,290
1758	14,383,248
1759	12,793,412
1760	13,311,674
1761	13,354,448

65,768,072 Tot. which is 13,153,614 *per An.*

1762	13,476,366
1763	13,110,858
1764	13,187,109
1765	14,757,353
1766	17,941,229

72,472,915 Tot. which is 14,494,583 *per An.*

1767	16,500,755
1768	15,249,248
1769	16,496,271
1770	18,195,087
1771	20,622,217

87,063,578 Tot. which is 17,612,715 *per An.*

| 1772 | 19,171,771 |
| 1773 | 17,896,994 |

Total

Total Quantities of Britiſh and Iriſh L I N ᴇ N s exported from England and Scotland from Jan. 1757 to Jan. 1774 with the Bounties paid each Year thereon.

	Britiſh.	Iriſh. Yds.	Bounty.		
1757	2,052,628	2,345,994	£.27353	11	4
1758	3,163,069	2,577,357	35832	1	10
1759	3,088,910	2,287,707	33584	4	1
1760	2,390,526	2,652,891	31471	12	1
1761	2,364,263	2,253,370	28855	14	4
Total	13,059,396	12,117,319	157097	3	8
per An.	2,611,879	2,423,463	31419	8	8
1762	2,598,524	3,460,453	37868	12	0
1763	3,801,421	2,953,324	42199	8	10
1764	3,744,861	2,175,004	36842	0	9
1765	3,340,263	1,964,579	33155	5	4
1766	3,648,247	2,224,547	36682	16	11
Total	17,133,316	12,777,907	186748	3	10
per An.	3,426,663	2,555,581	37349	12	9
1767	3,973,964	2,746,464	41971	11	9
1768	4,295,949	2,827,544	44517	18	11
1769	4,606,235	2,503,871	44086	5	1
1770	4,806,184	3,501,712	51901	10	1
1771	6,650,879	4,245,553	62203	14	5
Total	24,333,211	15,825,144	244681	6	3
per An.	4,866,642	3,165,028	48936	5	3
1772	8,479,408	3,508,827	61038	6	0
1773	7,908,554	2,752,999	53673	17	1

The above Account of Britiſh and Iriſh Linens exported includes only ſuch as are entitled to the Bounty, a very conſiderable Quantity is exported above 18 d. a Yard, of which no account is furniſhed from the Cuſtom-Houſe.

Sundry

Sundry STATES and OBSERVATIONS thereupon.

Exports from England to Holland from 1762 to 1766 inclufive, Foreign, *viz.* all the Eaft, Weft-India and
North-American Commodities to

Holland,	£. 4,820,412	4	2
Ditto to Germany,	5,276,758	7	0

Total from 1762 to 1766,	£. 10,097,170	11	2

Foreign as above from 1767 to 1771,

To Holland,	£. 4,854,331	9	3
Ditto to Germany,	4,393,547	3	10

Total from 1767 to 1771,	9,247,878	13	1

Decreafe in the Foreign,	£. 849,291	18	1

All in the Export to Germany, with £. 33,919 5 1 more,
the Export to Holland having increafed to that
Amount.

BRITISH Manufacture and Produce, the latter Lead,
Tin, Coals, Salt, &c. of trifling Value to the whole,
exported from 1762 to 1766 inclufive,

To Holland,	£. 4,868,221	5	5
Germany,	5,375,659	19	7

	£. 10,243,881	5	0

From 1767 to 1771. - - - -

To Holland,	£. 3,540,631	13	8
Germany,	2,540,405	18	9

Total from 1767 to 1771,	6,081,037	12	5

Decreafe in the Britifh,	£. 4,162,843	12	7
Ditto Foreign as on Page one,	849,291	18	1

Total of both,	£. 5,012,135	10	8

At a Medium of thefe laft five Years
£. 1,002,427 2 2 *per Ann.*

N. B.

N. B. Dec. in the Brit. to Germany, £. 2,835,254 0 10
    Ditto,   Foreign to ditto,   883,211 3 2
Total Decrease to Holland,   1,293,670 6 8

                       £. 5,012,135 10 8

Nearly ¾ to Germany direct,
But ¼ to Holland direct.
Although upon a Medium for 20 Years the Exports to
Holland have exceeded the Exports to Germany.

N. B. The Total of Exports to Germany and Holland
from 1762 to 1766 is about,   £. 20,340,000
Or, £. 4,068,000 at a Medium *per Ann.*
Ditto from 1767 to 1771 about,   15,330,000
Or, £. 3,066,000, *per Ann.* which makes above
£. 1,000,000 *per Ann.* Loss, yet in this State of de-
cline still exhibits an Export of the last mentioned
Sum, *viz.*   £. 3,066,000
The Imports from these Countries for ten Years back are
given in at about 1,090,000 *per Ann.*
Balance in favour of Great Britain,   £, 1,976,000
    State of the Linen exported from Ireland, and of Linen
stampt for Sale in Scotland in the above Periods, *viz.*
From 1762 to 1766, 141,418,328 *Yds.* Val. £.8,347,043
At a Medium of these Five
    Years, 28,283,665 *Yards.*
From 1767 to 1771, 166,866,870 *Yds.* Val. 10,855,528
At a Medium of these five
    Years, 33,373,374 *Yards.*

Annual Increase of Linens at a Medium
in the last Period about 5,000,000 *Yds.* Val. £. 325,276
Annual Decrease in the Exports to Holland
    and Germany to the Value of   £. 1,000,000
    N. B. Of the said decrease in the Exports £. 800,000
falls on Manufacture.

    N. B. Since these Calculations were produced, an Ac-
count hath been laid before Parliament, distinguishing
the different heads of export ; whereby it appears, that
British Produce, particularly Coal, is estimated higher
                           than

In Foreign Goods and Merchandize   850,000

British Produce,   662,000

Do. Manufacture,   ———

✳✳✳✳✳✳✳✳✳✳✳✳✳✳✳✳✳✳✳✳✳✳✳✳

A S P E E C H

Introductory to the

P R O P O S A L S

Laid before the ANNUITANTS of

Meff. DOUGLAS, HERON and Co.

AT THE

KING's-ARMS Tavern, Cornhill, on the
Ninth of *February*, 1774.

✳✳✳✳✳✳✳✳✳✳✳✳✳✳✳✳✳✳✳✳✳✳✳✳

A SPEECH.

LADIES and GENTLEMEN,

YOU are called together by virtue of an
advertisement, inviting the Annuitants of
Meff. Douglas, Heron and Co. to meet at this
place, and receive Propofals for the Redemp-
tion of their Annuities.

LADIES and GENTLEMEN,

You have conferred upon me the honour of
prefiding among you in this chair, where I
appear before you in a double capacity : Firft,
as an Annuitant myfelf; fecondly, as one de-
firous to contribute my part, however in-
confiderable to prevent any frefh wound to
Public Crredit, fo effentially hurt from June,
1772, and requiring a whole twelvemonth
after to revive.

Every one muft remember that fatal month
of June, when the firft link of that chain of
unnatural and forced circulation gave way, the
number of bankruptcies which enfued, and
the almoft total ftagnation of trade and ma-

nufacture

nufacture in every branch. In the midſt of
this calamity the unadviſed and raſh conduct
of the Air bank had out in London bills to
be provided for, amounting to ſix hundred
thouſand pounds.

Had their managers known the extent of
their own circulation, and the ſpecific periods
of its coming due, common forecaſt would
have made the neceſſary proviſion in time, and
enabled them to have ſold their annuities with
more facility at ten and eleven years purchaſe,
than at ſeven and eight, and conſequently
have produced a ſaving of more than one
hundred eighty thouſand pounds to that unfortunate company. But the want of all forecaſt brought upon them immediate preſſures,
inſurmountable by common means, and com-
pelled them to the recourſe of tendring uncommon advantages to lenders, that thoſe
who had money might be tempted to part
with it at a notice ſometimes not exceeding
eight-and-forty hours.

By this deſperate meaſure they raiſed at
different periods, in about three months, four
hundred and ſixty thouſand pounds, burdened
with

[69]

with an annual charge of sixty thousand pounds; an increase of drain beyond the faculties of Scotland to bear. To this four hundred and sixty thousand pounds they added from their own cash about sixty thousand pounds more, all they could possibly muster; and accordingly discharged five hundred and twenty thousand pounds value of their bills in London, but leaving still a circulation of fourscore thousand pounds to be struggled with. Their daily declining credit could endure this last conflict no longer than April 1773, when they were saved from bankruptcy, and Public Credit from another fatal blow by the interposition of Mr. Banks of Lincoln's-Inn, and of myself under him, who supplied that fourscore thousand pounds upon the security of landed estates in Scotland assigned to Sir William Henry Ashurst, the Lord Advocate of Scotland, the Solicitor-General of England, the Solicitor-General of Scotland, Mr. Banks, Mr. M'Konochie and myself, as trustees in behalf of the lenders, but with this express condition previously agreed, that Messrs. Douglas, Heron and

partners

partners fhould be diffolved as a banking
company. By this laft ftipulation the public
indeed was ferved, being no longer expofed to
a paper circulation of fo pernicious a nature.
However, the book and bond creditors, the
annuitants, and every partner of this unhap_
py company, were left in a precarious fituation from a weight of annual payment, to
which their monied faculties were unequal.

Many of the annuitants have been alarmed
at a fuggeftion that their annuities would be
made void in law, as ufurious bargains.
True it is, that infinuations of that fort have
been thrown out ; but it is as true that they
were heard with the higheft indignation by all
the worthy members of this fociety, and by
thofe noble perfonages in particular, who have
now ftept forth and taken upon themfelves
the manly part of winding up this unfortunate
bufinefs, the unadvifed, the blameable projeft
cf others : and were they convinced that thefe
contracts were actually voidable in law, yet
confcious of a tranfaction fo public, open and
fair, the noble perfonages rejeft the very
thought of fo mean a fubterfuge, and pledge
themfelves

themselves and their estates to the strict performance of their engagements. Heavy indeed will be the loss sustained by these noble Dukes; but probity can deduce good out of evil. Without this severe trial they never could have found so striking an occasion of evincing to mankind, how much the dignity and lustre derived from honour and rectitude are superior to rank, title and fortune. The one begins life with the early acquisition of glory, resulting from honesty, that supreme gift of God. The other will close his term with a last and greatest exertion of his long approved integrity, which hath ever obtained universal love and esteem, and will accompany his venerable head to the grave.

It was jointly with them only and directly on the single principle of supporting Public Credit, and relieving so many distressed and alarmed individuals, that I have lent my best assistance. Solicited and authorized by them, I now appear in their behalf before this respectable Assembly with proposals, which, whether accepted or rejected by you, will demonstrate the upright intentions of these deserving, ferving and virtuous Noblemen ; whom, as an independent man, I do not court ; but to whofe merit, as an honeft man, I muft do common juftice : and I have done no more.

Ladies and Gentlemen,

The fubject before you is of a public nature ; I have no fecrets about it : put to me what queftions you pleafe ; I will anfwer to the beft of my knowledge and information.

N. B. The propofals, which have been fince fo well underftood by the public, were unanimoufly agreed to, by a very numerous meeting of annuitants ; and the two original propofals, which were figned at the meeting, are left, one at Mr. Glover's in Martin's-lane, Cannon-ftreet, the other at Mr. Mayne's in Jermyn-ftreet, for fuch annuitants as pleafe to fubfcribe.

F I N I S.

www.ingramcontent.com/pod-product-compliance
Lightning Source LLC
Chambersburg PA
CBHW021529270326
41930CB00008B/1167